UN
COMMON

STUDY GUIDE

For foreign and subsidiary rights, contact the author.

Cover design by: Joe DeLeon

ISBN: 978-1-950718-67-2   1 2 3 4 5 6 7 8 9 10

Printed in the United States of America

UN COMMON

LEADERSHIP LESSONS FROM AROUND THE GLOBE

CALEB WEHRLI

STUDY GUIDE

CONTENTS

Beyond Common

"Uncommon impacts are made by common people who choose to live each and every day from the reality that Jesus lives within them."

Read Chapter 1: "Beyond Common," in *Uncommon*, reflect on the questions and discuss your answers with your study group.

What are several areas as a leader in which you're believing God to grow you through this book study?

_____

_____

_____

_____

_____

_____

The author's definition of "uncommon" is "remarkably great." What is your definition?

_____

_____

_____

_____

_____

_____

Matthew 5:14-16 (NIV):

"You are the light of the world. A town built on a hill cannot be hidden. Neither do people light a lamp and put it under a bowl. Instead they put it on its stand, and it gives light to everyone in the house. In the same way, let your light shine before others, that they may see your good deeds and glorify your Father in heaven."

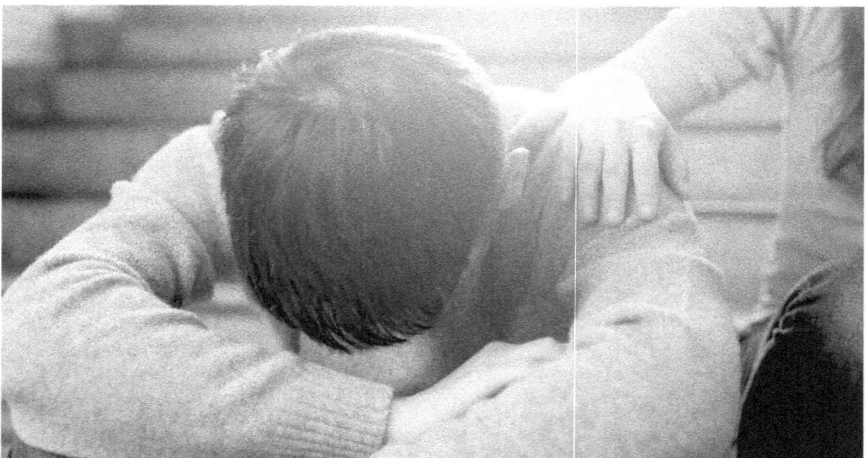

What parts of your life are uncommon? How do you feel about them?

_____

_____

_____

_____

_____

_____

_____

When you think of people who have lived uncommon lives, who do you think of? What strikes you as remarkable about these people?

_____

_____

_____

_____

_____

_____

_____

If you allowed Him to, what areas of your life would God make uncommon?

_____

_____

_____

_____

_____

_____

_____

"But you are a chosen people, a royal priest- hood, a holy nation, God's spe- cial posses- sion, that you may declare the praises of him who called you out of dark- ness into his won- derful light. Once you were not a people, but now you are the people of God; once you had not received mercy, but now you have received mercy." —1 Peter 2:9-10 (NIV)

What's holding you back from letting God upgrade your belief system and faith level?

_____

_____

_____

_____

_____

_____

_____

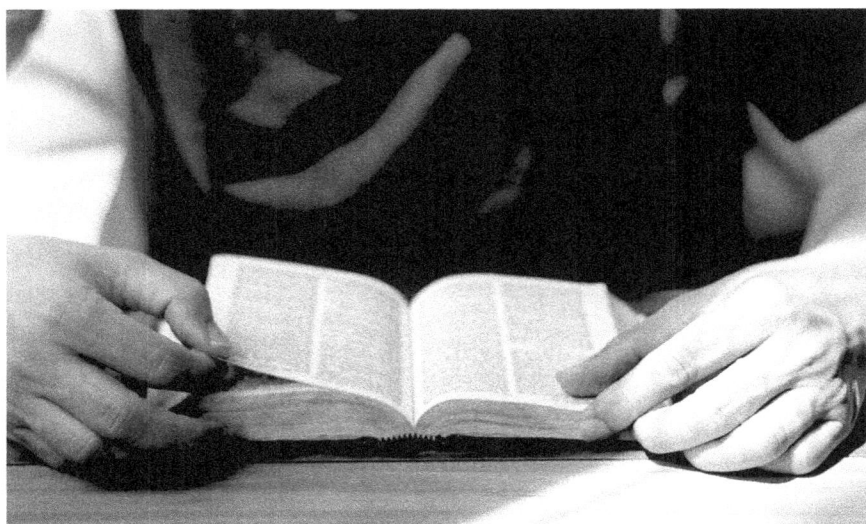

chapter 2

Uncommon Availability

"If you'll make yourself available, without a doubt God will make you capable."

READING TIME

Read Chapter 2: "Uncommon Availability," in *Uncommon*, reflect on the questions and discuss your answers with your study group.

When have you made yourself available in a new environment and found yourself completely changed as a result?

_____

_____

_____

_____

_____

_____

_____

What role do people play in making themselves capable of Kingdom work?

_____

_____

_____

_____

_____

_____

When have you found yourself incapable of doing something you thought you were completely qualified for? What do you think caused you to be unsuccessful?

_____

_____

_____

_____

_____

_____

When have you been surprised at your success? How can these successes be attributed to God's having deposited His limitless Kingdom resources into you?

_____

_____

_____

_____

_____

_____

How do you show your uncommon availability through the way you use your time, talent, and treasure? What people and purposes have you found on the other side of your decision to surrender these things?

_____

_____

_____

_____

_____

_____

_____

How can we see God's divine interruptions as opportunities to make an impact on the lives of those in our path?

_____

_____

_____

_____

_____

_____

_____

Uncommon Attitude

"*When we allow our attitudes to be controlled by what God says instead of what we see, things start to shift.*"

READING TIME

Read Chapter 3: "Uncommon Attitude," in *Uncommon*, reflect on the questions and discuss your answers with your study group.

In what areas has attitude been a constant challenge for you? Why do you think this is?

_____

_____

_____

_____

_____

_____

Do you agree with this statement? "You may not be able to control your surroundings or your circumstances, but you can always dictate what your response will be." Why or why not?

_____

_____

_____

_____

_____

REFLECT ON

Philippians 4:8-9 and how it might influence one's attitude:

Finally, brothers and sisters, whatever is true, whatever is noble, whatever is right, whatever is pure, whatever is lovely, whatever is admirable—if anything is excellent or praiseworthy—think about such things. Whatever you have learned or received or heard from me, or seen in me—put it into practice. And the God of peace will be with you.

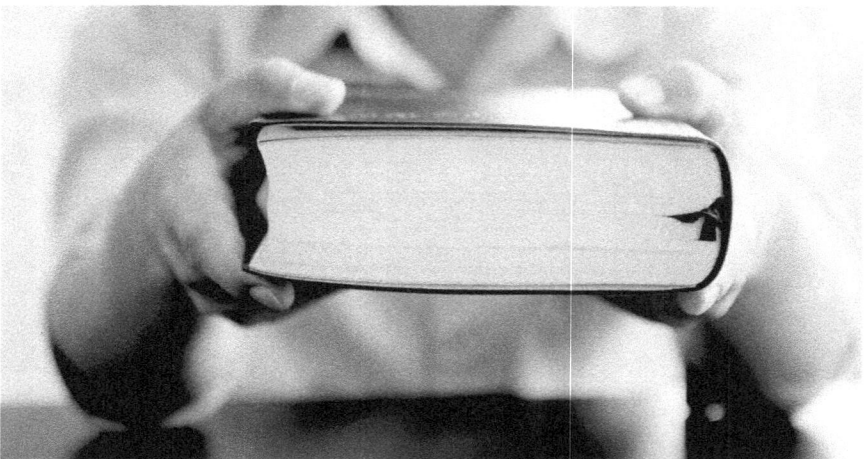

How would you encourage someone who truly felt at a loss to influence his or her own attitude?

_____

_____

_____

_____

_____

_____

_____

What does it look like when one's attitude is based on Christ's reality inside of a person, instead of the fear and uncertainty of the world?

_____

_____

_____

_____

_____

_____

_____

Trace one of your disappointments back to the specific moment that caused it. How could you change the way you look at that moment so that it only becomes a "bump" in the road on this amazing journey God has for you?

_____
_____
_____
_____
_____
_____
_____

Think of a situation you're experiencing that requires an uncommon attitude. How specifically can you pray, rely on the Spirit for strength, and praise in this situation so that discouragement doesn't take hold?

_____
_____
_____
_____
_____
_____
_____

Uncommon Language

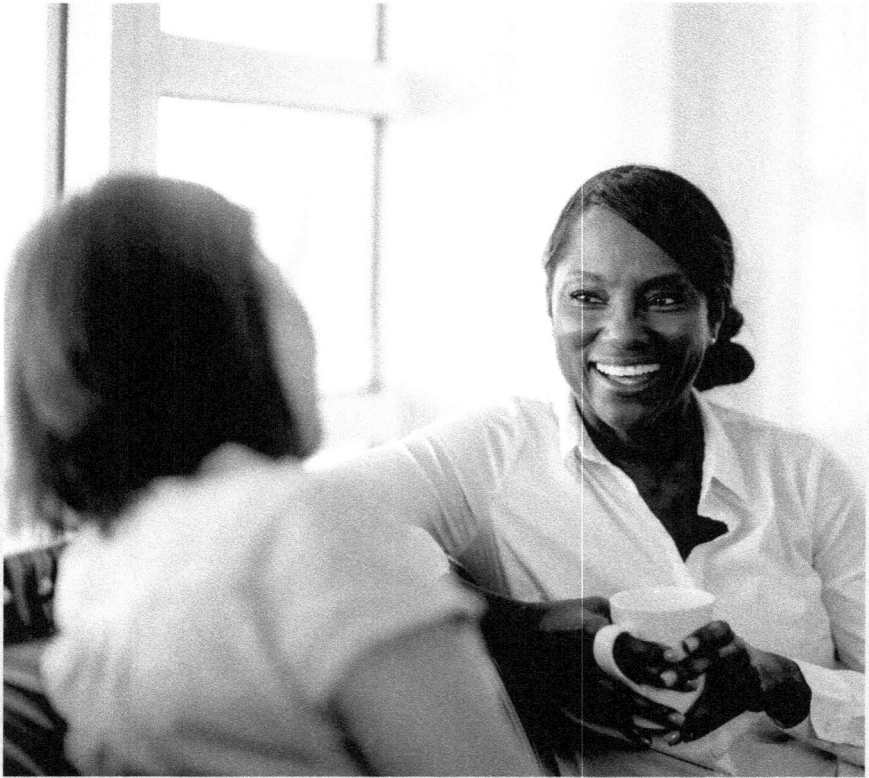

"Our words can produce miracles—and not just in our bodies, but also in our relationships, in our finances, in our health, and in every part of our life that we choose."

Read Chapter 4: "Uncommon Language," in *Uncommon*, reflect on the questions and discuss your answers with your study group.

What has been your life-long—from childhood until the present—experience with the power of words?

_____

_____

_____

_____

_____

_____

_____

What truths do you see in the analogy of words spoken as seeds cultivated in people's lives?

_____

_____

_____

_____

_____

_____

_____

REFLECT ON

Mark 11:20-24 (NKJV):

Now in the morning, as they passed by, they saw the fig tree dried up from the roots. And Peter, remembering, said to Him, "Rabbi, look! The fig tree which You cursed has withered away."

So Jesus answered and said to them, "Have faith in God. For assuredly, I say to you, whoever says to this mountain, 'Be removed and be cast into the sea,' and does not doubt in his heart, but believes that those things he says will be done, he will have whatever he says. Therefore I say to you, whatever things you ask when you pray, believe that you receive them, and you will have them."

What situation(s) are you dealing with for which you have no uncommon words to speak? How can you implement the author's directive, "If you don't know what to say, let God speak for you. Grab your Bible and write down what He has to say about your life and your future"?

_____

_____

_____

_____

_____

_____

_____

_____

_____

How can a person reconcile what he or she sees with what he or she says? What place does visual reality have in spiritual reality when it comes to a person's spoken (common or uncommon) words?

_____

_____

_____

_____

_____

_____

_____

_____

_____

_____

_____

"Just as focusing on yesterday's great moments can steal from today, so can over-focusing on today's challenges steal our tomorrow."

What does it look like when a person walks down the road of fear? How about the road of faith? Which do you most often trod?

_____
_____
_____
_____
_____
_____
_____
_____
_____
_____
_____

How can a person respond when accused of being naïve because he or she chooses to only speak uncommon words?

_____
_____
_____
_____
_____
_____
_____
_____
_____
_____
_____

Uncommon Generosity

*"Generosity is at the core of who Christ is.
His whole life speaks of sacrificial generosity.
He wants it to be at our core, too."*

READING TIME

Read Chapter 5: "Uncommon Generosity," in *Uncommon*, reflect on the questions and discuss your answers with your study group.

Think of a time Jesus took what you offered and multiplied it in a great way, like the boy with the five loaves and two fishes. What happened?

_____

_____

_____

_____

_____

_____

Do you agree with the following statement? "The only direct control we have over our future is the seed we sow in the present through generosity." Why or why not?

_____

_____

_____

_____

_____

REFLECT ON

Luke 21:1-4 (NKJV):

And He looked up and saw the rich putting their gifts into the treasury, and He saw also a certain poor widow putting in two mites. So He said, "Truly I say to you that this poor widow has put in more than all; for all these out of their abundance have put in offerings for God, but she out of her poverty put in all the livelihood that she had."

What is in your hand to give? What are you holding onto that God wants you to be generous with?

_____

_____

_____

_____

_____

_____

_____

How could you encourage someone wrestling with disappointment because it seems like his or her generosity will not be rewarded here on earth?

_____

_____

_____

_____

_____

_____

_____

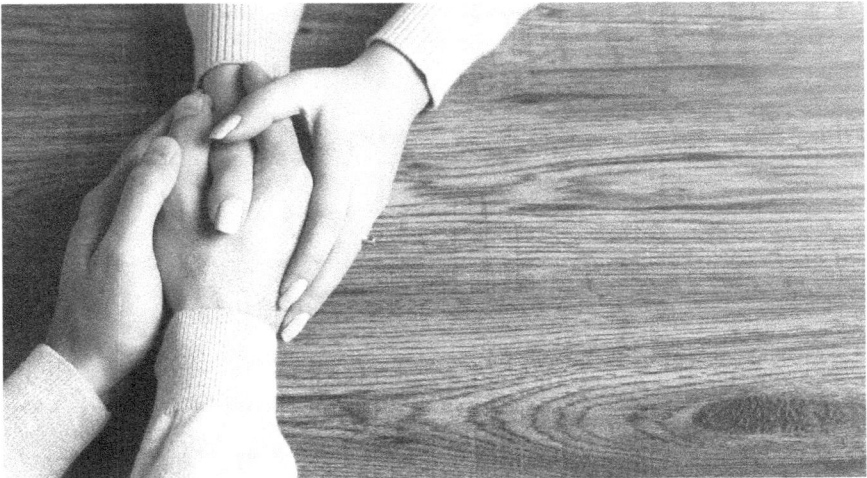

"When I choose to give individually or collectively with my church family, we become the hands and feet of Jesus, and I feel fully alive."

How does living with uncommon generosity change the lens through which you see life?

_____

_____

_____

_____

_____

_____

_____

_____

_____

_____

_____

As Christ followers, how we can love generously like Christ did? What does it look like to "put love into practice"?

_____

_____

_____

_____

_____

_____

_____

_____

_____

_____

_____

chapter 6

Uncommon Vision

"When we live...with uncommon vision, our lives will look and feel different, not just to ourselves, but also to those around us."

When has your journey required uncommon vision? What did the natural look like? What did it look like with your eyes closed?

_____

_____

_____

_____

_____

Do you agree with the following statement? "People with uncommon vision see promises instead of problems. They see opportunities in obstacles. They see supernatural intervention in the middle of natural challenges." Why or why not?

_____

_____

_____

_____

_____

_____

REFLECT ON

2 Corinthians 2:8-10 (ESV):

None of the rulers of this age understood this, for if they had, they would not have crucified the Lord of glory. But, as it is written, "What no eye has seen, nor ear heard, nor the heart of man imagined, what God has prepared for those who love him"— these things God has revealed to us through the Spirit. For the Spirit searches everything, even the depths of God.

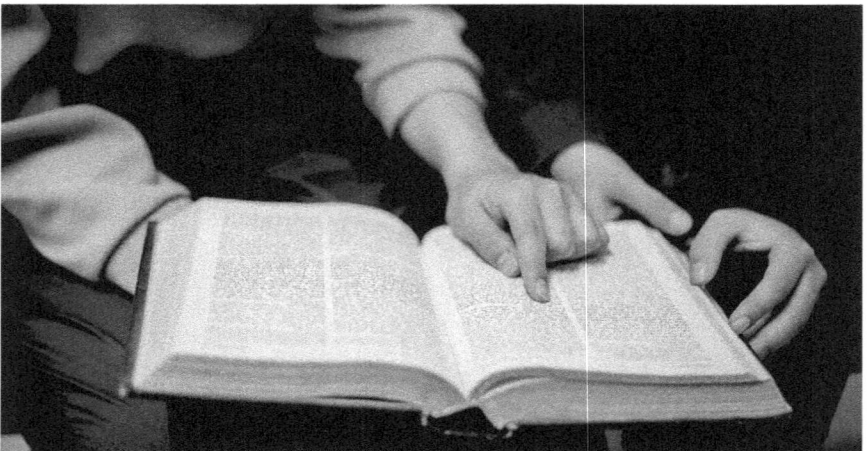

In which area of your life do you need to live on purpose so that you have greater precision in the direction your life is taking?

_____

_____

_____

_____

_____

_____

_____

How can the following help you begin to see what God sees for you?

God's Word _____

_____

_____

_____

_____

God's Presence _____

_____

_____

_____

_____

God's House _____

_____

_____

_____

_____

"Sometimes, we think we've lost the passion for our marriage, family or career, when in reality all we've lost is our vision. If we'll get our vision clear again, our passion will resurface."

What would be the benefits of developing uncommon vision in your life?

_____

_____

_____

_____

_____

_____

_____

_____

_____

Uncommon Pursuit

"It was important to me, so I chased it with everything that I had. It didn't matter how much I had to endure."

READING TIME

Read Chapter 7: "Uncommon Pursuit," in *Uncommon*, reflect on the questions and discuss your answers with your study group.

What has been the greatest pursuit in your life up until now?

_____

_____

_____

_____

_____

In your attempt to know God, how have you followed the words of Jeremiah 29:13 (NIV), "You will seek me and find me when you seek me with all your heart," and Matthew 6:33 (NIV), "But seek first his kingdom and his righteousness, and all these things will be given to you as well"?

_____

_____

_____

_____

_____

_____

How have you used your influence to further the Kingdom of God?

_____

_____

_____

_____

_____

_____

_____

How would people live differently if they lived lives of uncommon pursuit—with the end in mind?

_____

_____

_____

_____

_____

_____

Uncommon Faith

"It's only when we realize that we aren't good
enough that we can accept that God is. And it's
only when we accept God's goodness that He can
work on our behalf like He wants to. It's only then
that He can move us beyond our limitations."

READING TIME

Read
Chapter 8:
"Uncommon
Faith," in
Uncommon,
reflect on the
questions
and discuss
your answers
with your
study group.

How can you draw comfort from the lives of Moses, David, and Rahab— how do these stories show that God can and will use your life?

_____

_____

_____

_____

_____

_____

How would you encourage someone struggling to balance "You're not good enough" with "You're not good enough—apart from Christ"?

_____

_____

_____

_____

_____

_____

REFLECT ON

You need to persevere so that when you have done the will of God, you will receive what he has promised. For, "In just a little while, he who is coming will come and will not delay." And, "But my righteous one will live by faith. And I take no pleasure in the one who shrinks back." But we do not belong to those who shrink back and are destroyed, but to those who have faith and are saved.

What has God called you to do that you feel unqualified for—that will require uncommon faith to accomplish?

_____
_____
_____
_____
_____
_____
_____

Do you agree with the following statement? "The enemy can attack our minds, but he can't touch our hearts." Why or why not?

_____
_____
_____
_____
_____
_____

Uncommon Love

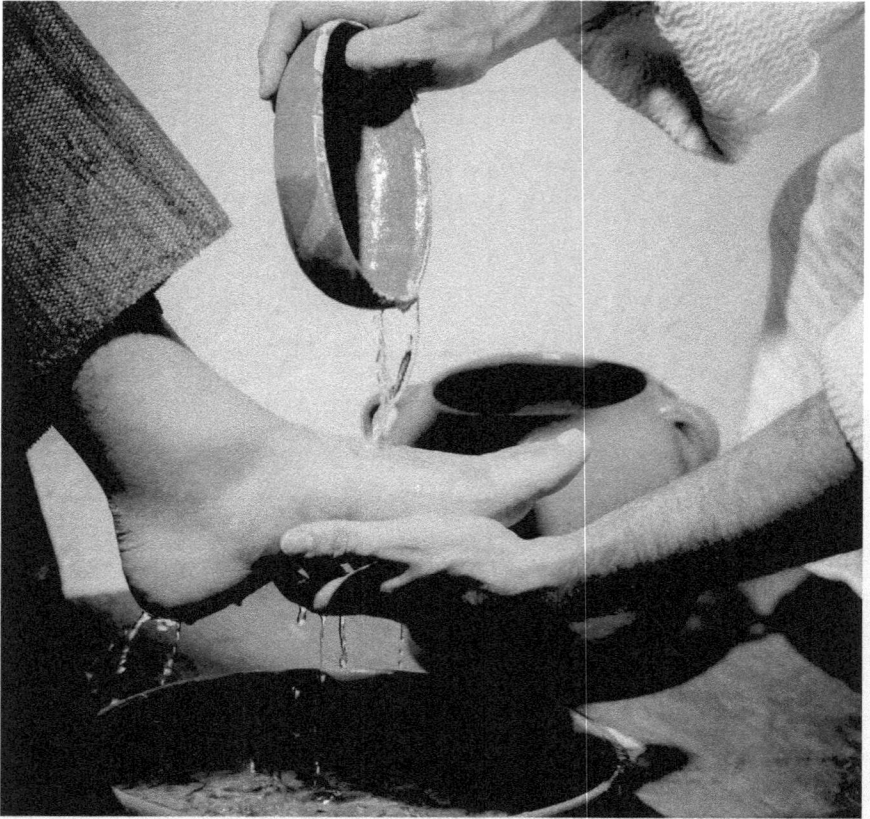

"I think it goes without saying that the best demonstration of uncommon love is Jesus himself."

Read Chapter 9: "Uncommon Love," in *Uncommon*, reflect on the questions and discuss your answers with your study group.

Which things or people in your life are easy to love? Which challenge you?

_____
_____
_____
_____
_____
_____
_____

When has the Lord asked you love daringly, bravely, and constantly? How did you do it?

_____
_____
_____
_____
_____
_____
_____

REFLECT ON

Ephesians 3:17-21:

I pray that you, being rooted and established in love, may have power, together with all the saints, to grasp how wide and long and high and deep is the love of Christ, and to know this love that surpasses knowledge—that you may be filled to the measure of all the fullness of God. Now to him who is able to do immeasurably more than all we ask or imagine, according to His power that is at work within us....

"He truly
loves
everyone,
without
condition.
He doesn't
give to get.
He just gives
to give."

Do you agree with the following statements? "The first thing for us to remember is simply to love the one in front of us," and, "We must put our compassion into action because love doesn't just sit around." Why or why not?

_____

_____

_____

_____

_____

_____

_____

_____

_____

_____

_____

Uncommon Peace

"I have discovered that God wants to upgrade our entire lives. He wants us to live as overcomers. He doesn't want us to succumb to our circumstances but to walk in victory each and every day."

READING TIME

Read Chapter 10: "Uncommon Peace," in *Uncommon*, reflect on the questions and discuss your answers with your study group.

What do you think of when you hear the word "upgrade"? What would a "peace upgrade" look like in your life?

_____

_____

_____

_____

_____

Write down every challenge, trial, or issue you're experiencing currently. What has caused you stress, or made you feel confused? Where is fear entering your heart? Now, next to each one, write the words, "... BUT God is greater."

_____

_____

_____

_____

_____

_____

John 16:32-33:

"A time is coming and in fact has come when you will be scattered, each to your own home. You will leave me all alone. Yet I am not alone, for my Father is with me. I have told you these things, so that in me you may have peace. In this world you will have trouble. But take heart! I have overcome the world."

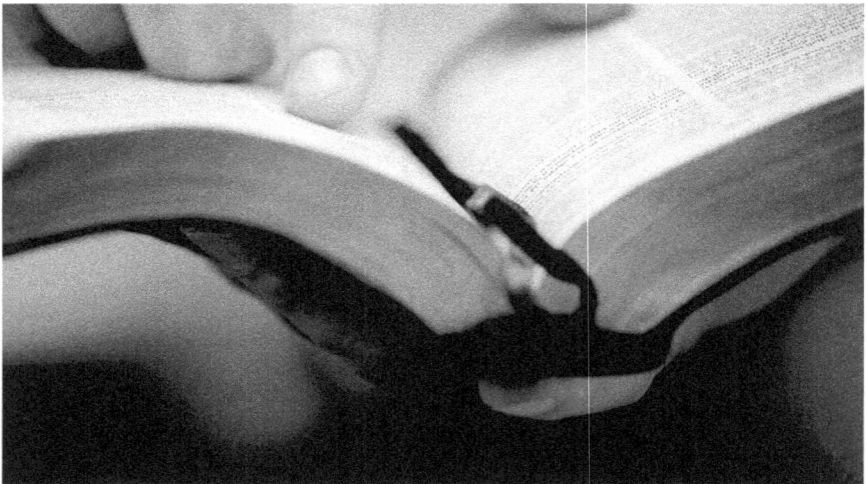

SHARE YOUR STORY

"You simply
have to have
courage
in order
to walk
into your
destiny."

Do you agree with this statement? "With God, uncertainty is nothing more than a blank slate reminding me that anything is still possible." Why or why not?

_____

_____

_____

_____

_____

_____

_____

Think of an instance of great uncertainty in your life. What was it about that situation that made it so daunting?

_____

_____

_____

_____

_____

_____

_____

How has God's peace upgraded your confidence, clarity, and courage?

_____

_____

_____

_____

_____

_____

Uncommon Power

"While salvation changes our eternity, discovering the power of the Holy Spirit changes our lives on earth."

Read
Chapter 11:
"Uncommon
Power," in
Uncommon,
reflect on the
questions
and discuss
your answers
with your
study group.

What is your understanding of the Trinity?
What role does the Holy Spirit play in it?

_____

_____

_____

_____

_____

_____

Do you agree with this statement? "When
God fills us with His Spirit, we gain the
opportunity to lead supernatural lives." Why
or why not?

_____

_____

_____

_____

_____

_____

_____

REFLECT ON

Romans 8:9-11(NIV):

You, however, are not in the realm of the flesh but are in the realm of the Spirit, if indeed the Spirit of God lives in you. And if anyone does not have the Spirit of Christ, they do not belong to Christ. But if Christ is in you, then even though your body is subject to death because of sin, the Spirit gives life because of righteousness. And if the Spirit of him who raised Jesus from the dead is living in you, he who raised Christ from the dead will also give life to your mortal bodies because of his Spirit who lives in you.

How have you seen the Holy Spirit's presence enable you to walk in His will, to share Christ with boldness, and to live a supernatural life?

_____

_____

_____

_____

_____

_____

_____

How would you encourage someone who just can't wrap his or her natural mind around our supernatural God?

_____

_____

_____

_____

_____

_____

Uncommon Character

"Building a deeper foundation doesn't just build stronger buildings, it builds stronger lives as well. This foundation can be the difference between your success and failure."

Read
Chapter 12:
"Uncommon
Chaacter," in
Uncommon,
reflect on the
questions
and discuss
your answers
with your
study group.

When you think of the word "character,"
what comes to mind?

_____

_____

_____

_____

_____

_____

_____

How is a person's character different from
his or her reputation? Which is more valuable to you? Which is more valuable to God?

_____

_____

_____

_____

_____

_____

REFLECT ON

Psalm 1:1-3 (NIV):

Blessed is the one who does not walk in step with the wicked or stand in the way that sinners take or sit in the company of mockers, but whose delight is in the law of the LORD, and who meditates on his law day and night. That person is like a tree planted by streams of water, which yields its fruit in season and whose leaf does not wither—whatever they do prospers.

Do you agree with this statement? "Adversity will never decide your character; it will reveal it." Why or why not?

_____

If you were to take the Character Challenge, what would you notice about your environment? How is it affecting your fruit?

_____

What changes do you need to make so that uncommon character is one of your strongest traits?

_____

Uncommon Obedience

"Sometimes, I think we are waiting for God to work when He is waiting on our obedience."

READING
TIME

Read
Chapter 13:
"Uncommon
Obedience,"in
Uncommon,
reflect on the
questions
and discuss
your answers
with your
study group.

What do you have the hardest time trusting
God with? Why do you think this is?

_____

_____

_____

_____

_____

_____

_____

Who do you know who has exhibited
uncommon obedience during his or her life-
time? What has that person done?

_____

_____

_____

_____

_____

_____

REFLECT ON

King Saul's actions in 1 Samuel 15:21-23 (NIV):

"The soldiers took sheep and cattle from the plunder, the best of what was devoted to God, in order to sacrifice them to the LORD your God at Gilgal." But Samuel replied: "Does the LORD delight in burnt offerings and sacrifices as much as in obeying the LORD? To obey is better than sacrifice, and to heed is better than the fat of rams. For rebellion is like the sin of divination, and arrogance like the evil of idolatry. Because you have rejected the word of the LORD, he has rejected you as king."

SHARE YOUR STORY

"We start out trusting him, but soon enough, we get comfortable with our own abilities and stop seeking His counsel daily. Sadly, like the ruined carpet, it will catch up with us eventually."

Do you agree with this statement? "The truth about trust is that it doesn't just prove itself through attitude; it also proves itself through action." Why or why not?

_____
_____
_____
_____
_____
_____
_____

What are you facing today that requires the uncommon trust that leads to obedience? What has God asked you to believe? What has He asked you to do?

_____
_____
_____
_____
_____
_____

chapter 14

Uncommon Grace

*"[God's grace] is the greatest gift we will ever receive,
and not just because it changes our lives for eternity—
but because it continues to change our lives today."*

Read
Chapter 14:
"Uncommon
Grace," in
Uncommon,
reflect on the
questions
and discuss
your answers
with your
study group.

Which aspect of God's grace are you most
grateful for?

_____

_____

_____

_____

_____

_____

_____

Are you on the grace road today? Or have
you taken your own path? Based on your
answer, what is your next step?

_____

_____

_____

_____

_____

_____

_____

REFLECT ON

John 1:15-18 (NIV):

(John testified concerning him. He cried out, saying, "This is the one I spoke about when I said, 'He who comes after me has surpassed me because he was before me.'") Out of his fullness we have all received grace in place of grace already given. For the law was given through Moses; grace and truth came through Jesus Christ. No one has ever seen God, but the one and only Son, who is himself God and is in closest relationship with the Father, has made him known.

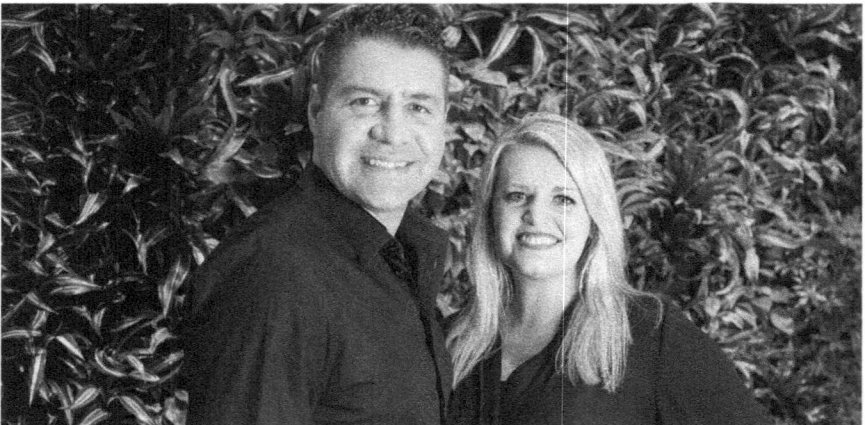

How does the fact that Jesus grew in grace (Luke 2:52) cause you to accept grace and extend it to yourself and others?

_____

_____

_____

_____

_____

_____

Do you agree with the following statement? "The beautiful thing about pain is that it always has a purpose." Why or why not?

_____

_____

_____

_____

_____

_____

How is God challenging you to focus, extend grace, and take action?

_____

_____

_____

_____

_____

_____

www.ingramcontent.com/pod-product-compliance
Lightning Source LLC
Chambersburg PA
CBHW020217090426
42734CB00008B/1108